TEAM SPIRIT®

SMART BOOKS FOR YOUNG FANS

THE HOUSTON TEXANS

BY
MARK STEWART

New Hanover County Public Library
201 Chestnut Street
Wilmington, North Carolina 28401

NORWOOD HOUSE PRESS
CHICAGO, ILLINOIS

Norwood House Press
P.O. Box 316598
Chicago, Illinois 60631

For information regarding Norwood House Press, please visit our website at:
www.norwoodhousepress.com or call 866-565-2900.

All photos courtesy of Getty Images except the following:
Icon SMI (4), Black Book Partners (7, 8, 11, 14, 17, 25, 36, 39),
Topps, Inc. (10, 15, 18, 20, 23, 35 all, 37, 38, 40, 41),
Sports Illustrated/TIME Inc. (33), Matt Richman (48).
Cover Photo: Icon SMI

The memorabilia and artifacts pictured in this book are presented for educational and informational purposes,
and come from the collection of the author.

Editor: Mike Kennedy
Designer: Ron Jaffe
Project Management: Black Book Partners, LLC.
Special thanks to Topps, Inc.

Library of Congress Cataloging-in-Publication Data

Stewart, Mark, 1960-
  The Houston Texans / by Mark Stewart. -- Rev. ed.
    p. cm. -- (Team spirit)
  Includes bibliographical references and index.
  Summary: "A revised Team Spirit Football edition featuring the Houston
Texans that chronicles the history and accomplishments of the team. Includes
access to the Team Spirit website which provides additional information and
photos"--Provided by publisher.
  ISBN 978-1-59953-524-1 (library edition : alk. paper) -- ISBN
978-1-60357-466-2 (ebook)
  1. Houston Texans (Football team)--History--Juvenile literature. I.
Title.
  GV956.H69S84 2012
  796.332'64097641411--dc23
                                        2012016226

Manufactured in the United States of America in North Mankato, Minnesota.
205N—082012

COVER PHOTO: Fans of the Texans get just as excited about a touchdown as the players do.

Table of Contents

ABOUT OUR GLOSSARY

In this book, there may be several words that you are reading for the first time. Some are sports words, some are new vocabulary words, and some are familiar words that are used in an unusual way. All of these words are defined on page 46. Throughout the book, sports words appear in **bold type**. Regular vocabulary words appear in ***bold italic type***.

Meet the Texans

Few fans in the United States love their football more than the people of Houston, Texas. Some follow high school football, some follow college football, and some follow *professional* football. Most know something about all three. No wonder the players on the Houston Texans love their city.

The Texans are Houston's second pro football team. The first, the Oilers, left in 1997 after 36 years there. The city seemed strangely empty without a **National Football League (NFL)** team. No one was surprised when the NFL returned to Houston a few years later.

This book tells the story of the Texans. They are one of the newest teams in football, but their fans have been following pro football for generations. That's another reason why the Texans love to play in Houston. They know a good effort will not go unnoticed—and a great play will make the whole stadium stand up and cheer.

The Texans celebrate a touchdown. They love to make their fans stand up and cheer.

Glory Days

When pro football arrived in Houston in 1960, sports fans there rejoiced. Some of the country's top high school and college players already sharpened their skills on the city's playing fields. The Houston Oilers completed the picture. For 36 seasons, they were one of America's most exciting teams. In 1997, the Oilers moved to Tennessee, where they became the Titans. Houston fans were in shock. They couldn't imagine a fall without the NFL.

For five seasons, Houston was without an NFL team. A group of investors led by Bob McNair worked hard to fix this problem. Finally, in 2002, the league expanded and placed a new team in Houston. The

LEFT: Owner Bob McNair poses with David Carr.
RIGHT: Aaron Glenn was a defensive leader of the Texans.

Texans were part of the **American Football Conference (AFC)**. One of the teams in their **division** was the Titans. Everyone knew this would turn into a great *rivalry*.

Houston's first coach was Dom Capers. He worked quickly to build a strong defense. Capers got good performances from players such as Aaron Glenn, Jamie Sharper, Gary Walker, Marcus Coleman, and Dunta Robinson. They helped the Texans earn a *reputation* as a hard-hitting team.

The offense looked for leadership from quarterback David Carr. Domanick Williams was the team's top running back. Houston's best player was Andre Johnson. He was a big receiver with

tremendous speed. In just his second season, he played in the **Pro Bowl**. When Johnson teamed with Jabar Gaffney, the Texans' passing game was hard to stop.

Houston got off to a great start in its very first game. The Texans hosted the Dallas Cowboys on a Sunday night. People all over Texas—and the nation—tuned in to watch. Carr put the Texans ahead with a

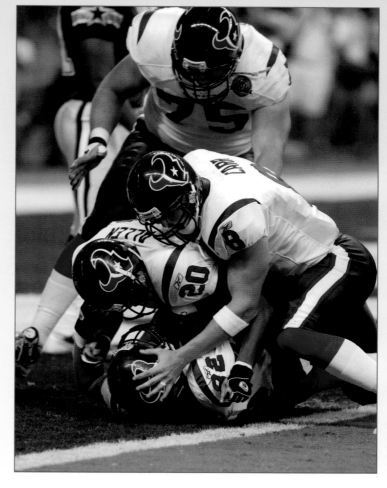

19-yard touchdown pass to Billy Miller. Houston's defense took over from there, and the Texans won, 19–10.

Thanks to their defense, the Texans played a lot of close games. But they lacked the experience to win in the final minutes. That began to change in 2007. Houston built an excellent defense around young stars DeMeco Ryans, Mario Williams, and Amobi Okoye.

LEFT: Andre Johnson's size and speed made him Houston's top player.
ABOVE: The Texans celebrate the winning touchdown against the Dallas Cowboys in 2002.

The offense, meanwhile, began to put points on the board after strong-armed quarterback Matt Schaub took over as the starter. He and Johnson developed into one of the league's most dangerous passing combinations. In 2007, the Texans finished with an 8–8 record. They matched that mark the following season. In 2009, Houston enjoyed its first winning season at 9–7.

The team set its sights on its next major goal: reaching the **playoffs**. They made that happen in 2011. By then, Houston had become one of the most feared teams in football. The Texans had two excellent running backs in Arian Foster and Ben Tate. They also had a group of sure-handed receivers that included Jacoby Jones. Neil Rackers was one of the league's most reliable kickers.

Houston was even better on defense. Brian Cushing led a group of hungry young stars, including Connor Barwin, Shaun Cody, J.J. Watt, and Antonio Smith. Defensive backs Johnathan Joseph and Jason Allen combined for eight **interceptions**.

Despite injuries to several key players, the Texans pushed forward and won the **AFC South** with a 10–6 record. They celebrated with

their fans after making the **postseason** for the first time. Houston continued to play well and came within a touchdown of reaching the **AFC Championship Game**. The fans were disappointed when the team fell short, but they felt great about the future. They knew a trip to the **Super Bowl** was not far away.

LEFT: This trading card shows Arian Foster breaking a tackle in 2010.
ABOVE: Brian Cushing helped the Texans win the AFC South in 2011.

Home Turf

When the Texans started in 2002, they also opened a new stadium. They still play there today. The stadium is part of a large sports and *convention* complex.

The Texans' stadium is impressive. It was built with a *retractable* roof, which rolls back in two five-piece sections from above the 50-yard line. The roof can open and close in as little as seven minutes. The Texans play on a grass field, which needs sunlight to stay in good shape. For this reason, the stadium roof is usually kept open. In 2004, Super Bowl XXXVIII was played in Houston.

BY THE NUMBERS

- The Texans' stadium has 71,054 seats.
- The stadium cost $352 million to build.
- At its fastest speed, the stadium roof can open at 35 feet per minute.

The roof is closed on the Texans' stadium for a game on a rainy afternoon.

Dressed for Success

The Texans are proud of their home state. In fact, they chose their team colors—red, white, and blue—as a salute to the Texas flag. Houston uses special versions of these colors known as Deep Steel Blue, Battle Red, and Liberty White.

The team *logo* also pays tribute to Texas. It is shaped like the head of a Texas bull. The logo has the same colors as the state flag and includes the famous five-pointed star. The points stand for pride, courage, strength, *tradition*, and independence.

For home games, the Texans usually wear blue jerseys. They

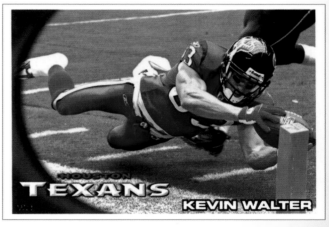

also have red jerseys that are saved for "Bull Red Day." In 2007, the Texans wore their red jerseys and red pants for the first time. That has proved to be a popular combination. On Bull Red Day, Houston fans dress in red to match the players.

LEFT: Jacoby Jones warms up in the team's white road uniform.
ABOVE: This trading card shows Kevin Walter wearing Houston's Bull Red Day uniform.

We Won!

When the 2011 season began, Houston football fans were more excited about the Texans than ever before. The previous year had been disappointing. Houston had finished 6–10 and missed the playoffs. However, some experts were now saying the team actually had a chance to reach the Super Bowl.

No one questioned the talent on Houston's roster. The team had

some of the best players in the NFL. Plus, the Texans had another advantage. They felt like they had something to prove. Sure enough, the team got off to a good start. They defeated the Indianapolis Colts and Miami Dolphins in their first two games.

Houston's season took a surprising turn over the next few weeks. The Texans hit a slump and lost three of four games. The pressure was on coach Gary Kubiak and quarterback Matt Schaub to get the team

back on track. They did just that. The Texans traveled to Tennessee and beat the Titans, 41–7.

From there, the team rolled to victories over the Jacksonville Jaguars, Cleveland Browns, and Tampa Bay Buccaneers. The Texans were playing great football, even without two of their top stars. Andre Johnson and Mario Williams both went down with serious injuries. Things got worse when Schaub was injured and the Texans learned that he was out for the year.

When a team suffers so much bad luck, one of two things can happen. The players either give up or they pull together and play even better. The Texans refused to make excuses. They went to Jacksonville and beat the Jaguars again. The good news was that Houston now had the best record in the AFC. The bad news was that

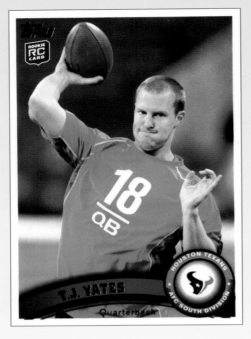

backup quarterback Matt Leinert was hurt in the game. Like Schaub, he would miss the rest of the season.

In the face of this challenge, Kubiak turned to an **untested** **rookie** named T.J. Yates to take over at quarterback. Yates came through in his first game. He survived a tremendous pass rush against the Atlanta Falcons and led the Texans to a 17–10 victory.

One week later, Yates was the hero again. He guided the Texans to an amazing comeback against the Cincinnati Bengals. With Houston trailing 19–13 late in the fourth quarter, Yates directed a 98-yard drive for the winning touchdown. The victory gave Houston its first-ever division title—and its first trip to the playoffs.

As luck would have it, the Texans hosted the Bengals in the first round of the playoffs. Fans in Houston could hardly wait for kickoff. The city had not seen an NFL postseason game since 1993, when the Oilers were in town. More than 70,000 fans filled the stadium. They were ready to cheer their hearts out.

The Bengals took an early lead, but the Texans knotted the score on a touchdown by Arian Foster. After the teams traded **field goals**,

rookie J.J. Watt intercepted a Cincinnati pass and ran it back for a touchdown to put Houston ahead 17–10.

In the second half, the Texans continued to play great defense. Yates threw a 40-yard touchdown pass to Johnson, and Foster scored again on a 42-yard run. The final score was 31–10. The Texans had their first postseason victory. Although they later fell short of their main goal—reaching the Super Bowl—they had taken an important first step toward their dream.

LEFT: This trading card shows T.J. Yates during his rookie season.
ABOVE: J.J. Watt gets a pat on the back from DeMeco Ryans after his interception and touchdown.

To be a true star in the NFL, you need more than fast feet and a big body. You have to be a "go-to guy"—someone the coach wants on the field at the end of a big game. Texans fans have had a lot to cheer about over the years, including these great stars …

THE PIONEERS

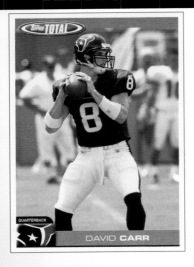

DAVID CARR

DAVID CARR   Quarterback

• BORN: 7/21/1979   • PLAYED FOR TEAM: 2002 TO 2006

In 2002, the Texans took David Carr with the first pick in the **draft**. He became their starting quarterback that season. Carr was a good leader and an accurate passer. In 2006, he topped the NFL by completing more than 68 percent of his passes.

JAMIE SHARPER   Linebacker

• BORN: 11/23/1974   • PLAYED FOR TEAM: 2002 TO 2004

Jamie Sharper was a tackling machine with Houston. In all, he made more than 400 tackles for the Texans. Sharper had the strength to bring down powerful running backs and the speed to chase after fast receivers.

DOMANICK WILLIAMS   Running Back

- BORN: 10/1/1980   • PLAYED FOR TEAM: 2003 TO 2005

Domanick Williams was the first player in NFL history to be named Rookie of the Week four weeks in a row. Williams rushed for more than 1,000 yards twice for the Texans.

DUNTA ROBINSON   Defensive Back

- BORN: 4/11/1982   • PLAYED FOR TEAM: 2004 TO 2009

In high school, Dunta Robinson played football and basketball and was a sprinter on the track team. He intercepted six passes as a rookie and had two **sacks** of **All-Pro** quarterback Peyton Manning.

MARIO WILLIAMS   Defensive Lineman

- BORN: 1/31/1985   • PLAYED FOR TEAM: 2006 TO 2011

In 2006, the Texans passed on hometown favorite Vince Young and drafted Mario Williams instead. In his second season, he set a team record with 14 sacks and was voted All-Pro. Williams made the Pro Bowl in 2008 and 2009.

DeMECO RYANS   Linebacker

- BORN: 7/28/1984   • PLAYED FOR TEAM: 2006 TO 2011

DeMeco Ryans made 12 tackles in his first game with Houston. Before long, he was known as one of the best linebackers in the league. Ryans was named the NFL's Defensive Rookie of the Year in 2006.

LEFT: David Carr   **ABOVE**: Mario Williams

ANDRE JOHNSON   Receiver

- BORN: 7/1/1981   • FIRST YEAR WITH TEAM: 2003

Andre Johnson became one of the league's most feared receivers with the Texans. He led the NFL in catches twice, in 2006 and again in 2008. From 2004 to 2010, Johnson made the Pro Bowl five times and was named an All-Pro twice.

OWEN DANIELS   Tight End

- BORN: 11/9/1982   • FIRST YEAR WITH TEAM: 2006

Owen Daniels was a good blocker and a reliable receiver. He caught 30 or more passes in each of his first six seasons with the Texans. Daniels was voted to the Pro Bowl in 2008, when he made 70 catches.

MATT SCHAUB   Quarterback

- BORN: 6/25/1981   • FIRST YEAR WITH TEAM: 2007

Matt Schaub waited patiently to become a starting quarterback in the NFL. He got his chance with the Texans in 2007. In 2009, he was picked to play in the Pro Bowl. That year, Schuab led the NFL with 396 completions and 4,770 passing yards. He also set a team record with 29 touchdown passes.

BRIAN CUSHING   Linebacker

- BORN: 1/24/1987   • FIRST YEAR WITH TEAM: 2009

In his first season, Brian Cushing had four sacks and four interceptions and also caused two **fumbles**. He was named Rookie of the Year and played in the Pro Bowl. Houston fans loved the way Cushing roamed all over the field to make tackles.

ARIAN FOSTER Running Back

- BORN: 9/24/1986   • FIRST YEAR WITH TEAM: 2009

Arian Foster was **overlooked** by many teams coming out of college. That changed after the first week of the 2010 season, when he exploded for 231 yards in a win over the Indianapolis Colts. Foster went on to lead the NFL in rushing with 1,616 yards. He was named to the Pro Bowl that year and the following season.

JOHNATHAN JOSEPH Defensive Back

- BORN: 4/16/1984   • FIRST YEAR WITH TEAM: 2011

The Texans signed Johnathan Joseph away from the Cincinnati Bengals in 2011. He quickly became one of the team's defensive stars. Joseph made an interception against his old team in the playoffs that season to help Houston win its first-ever postseason game.

J.J. WATT   Defensive End

- BORN: 3/22/1989
- FIRST YEAR WITH TEAM: 2011

The Texans drafted J.J. Watt to help energize their defense. He did exactly that in his rookie season. Watt got better and better as the year progressed. In the playoffs, he intercepted a pass and ran it back for a touchdown.

Defensive End

RIGHT: J.J. Watt

23

Calling the Shots

In the NFL, a team's first coach sets the tone for years to come. The Texans knew this when they chose Dom Capers to lead them in 2002. Capers had been the first coach of another **expansion club**, the Carolina Panthers. He helped assemble the Panthers in 1995, and a year later they were one of the league's best teams.

No one was more dedicated than Capers. He worked 16 to 18 hours a day and often slept in his office so he could get a quick start the next morning. Capers was a defensive genius. He knew how to blend the strengths of his players and how to hide their weaknesses. The Texans' defense surprised and confused opponents. It was known for its hard, physical play.

With that foundation in place, Houston turned to someone who could do the same thing for the offense. That coach was Gary Kubiak. He had been a high school football star in Houston and later a quarterback in the NFL for nine seasons. After his playing days, Kubiak worked as a coach with two legendary passers, Steve Young and John Elway.

Gary Kubiak led his hometown team to the AFC South title in 2011.

As the coach of the Texans, Kubiak built his offense around quarterback Matt Schaub and receiver Andre Johnson. They developed into one of the NFL's best passing duos. Arian Foster also became a great running back under Kubiak.

The Texans had their first winning season in 2009. The following season, however, the team took a step backward and finished 6–10. Kubiak added Wade Phillips to his staff to rebuild the defense. Kubiak focused on the offense. The Texans had their best season in 2011. Not only did they win their first AFC South crown, they also had the top-ranked defense in the NFL!

One Great Day

The draft is the first place most teams look to when they need to find a good player. In 2010, the Texans had a weak running game. Houston fans were excited when the team picked Ben Tate. He had run for more than 3,000 yards at Auburn University.

Unfortunately, disaster struck in training camp. Tate suffered a broken ankle and was lost for the year. The Texans had no choice but to ask Arian Foster to step into the starting role. Foster was not drafted after college. He joined the Houston **practice squad** in 2009 and was only added to the roster in November. Foster had run the ball just 54 times in his pro career.

Houston's 2010 season opener came against the powerhouse Indianapolis Colts. Over the years, Peyton Manning and his teammates had dealt the Texans many *humiliating* defeats. But something seemed different this day. Every time Foster touched the ball, he found room to run. He gained more than 40 yards on two different plays and also scored a 25-yard touchdown.

Arian Foster outruns the Indianapolis Colts on his way to a 231-yard day.

The Texans kept giving the ball to Foster, and he kept making big plays. On that day, he found the end zone three times and set a team record with 231 rushing yards. The sensational rookie led Houston to a 34–24 victory.

Foster's game against the Colts was truly a history-making event. Only one other player since 1933 had gained more yards on opening day. Foster proved his performance was for real when he went on to win the NFL's rushing crown that season. What happened to Tate? He recovered in 2011 to give the Houston running game an awesome one-two punch.

Legend Has It

Who once threw a football as the first pitch in a baseball game?

LEGEND HAS IT that Bob McNair did. On the day that McNair announced that Houston's new team would be called the Texans, he was invited to throw the traditional "first pitch" before a Houston Astros game. McNair walked out to the pitcher's mound, but he had a different idea. Instead of throwing a baseball, the Texans' owner tossed a football to home plate. The "catcher" was Astros owner Drayton McLane.

ABOVE: Bob McNair
RIGHT: Kris Brown

Which Texan was poetry in motion?

that Arian Foster was. In college, Foster studied **philosophy** and wrote lots of poetry. When he became a star for the Texans, his poems began finding their way onto the Internet. Fans thought they were great—and the experts agreed. In 2010, *The Sporting News* called Foster "The Most Interesting Man in the NFL."

Who had the "longest" leg in the NFL?

that Kris Brown did. Other kickers have made longer field goals, but no one booted more 50-yarders in the same game than Brown. In a 2007 contest against the Miami Dolphins, he kicked five field goals—including two successful attempts from 54 yards and one from 57 yards. Brown's 57-yarder won the game 22–19 with one second left.

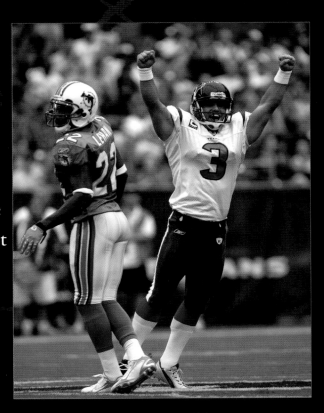

Defense often wins games in the NFL. The Texans found this out in their first season. Houston was hosting the Pittsburgh Steelers, a team that was famous for its defense. On this day, however, the Texans were even better.

The Houston defense made its first big play in the first quarter when quarterback Tommy Maddox fumbled the ball. Kenny Wright scooped it up and ran 40 yards for a touchdown. The next time the Steelers had the ball, Aaron Glenn intercepted a pass by Maddox and returned it 70 yards for a score.

The Steelers responded with two field goals to cut the lead to 14–6. Pittsburgh fans got ready to watch their team make a great comeback. The Steelers, however, continued to make mistakes. They fumbled a punt, and Kris Brown kicked a field goal to give the Texans a 17–6 lead. With two minutes left, Glenn intercepted another pass and raced 65 yards for his second touchdown of the day. Though the Texans had less than 50 yards in total offense, they were in control.

James Simmons celebrates a fumble recovery against the Pittsburgh Steelers.

The final score was 24–6. Pittsburgh had gained 422 yards but could not score a touchdown. Houston coach Dom Capers awarded the game ball to his defense. Houston quarterback David Carr joked afterward: "They should take the game ball they got and throw it at us!"

Team Spirit

A Texans game is like a big party, especially when the team wins. Houston fans love to make noise. Their favorite chant is, "We must protect this house!"

The loudest fans in Houston's stadium are often seated behind the north end zone. This area is called the "Bull Pen." People in these seats love Toro, the team's *mascot*. Toro—the Spanish word for "bull"—roams the field during games. He shares the sidelines with the Bull Pen Pep Band and the Houston cheerleaders.

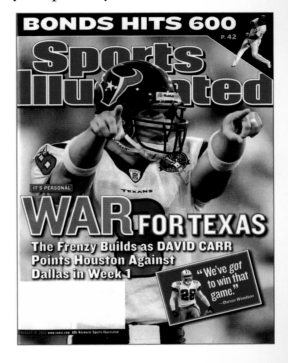

Before kickoff, fans throw big tailgate parties in the parking lot. Many families visit the Fanatic Fan Zone. After games, fans stay in their seats for the "5th Quarter"—a video review of the game, along with highlights from other NFL games.

LEFT: Andre Johnson visits the famous Bull Pen.   **ABOVE**: Houston fans gobbled up this issue of *Sports Illustrated* before the Texans' first game.

Timeline

T he Texans have had a lot to celebrate over the years. This timeline shows some of their greatest achievements.

2005
Kick returner Jerome Mathis is named All-Pro.

2002
The Texans play their first season.

1999
The NFL announces that Houston will get a new team.

2003
Aaron Glenn and Gary Walker start in the Pro Bowl.

2006
DeMeco Ryans is voted Defensive Rookie of the Year.

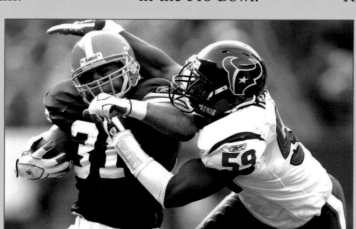

DeMeco Ryans tackles a Cleveland Browns runner.

Mario
Williams

Ben Tate
helped the
Texans make
the playoffs
in 2011.

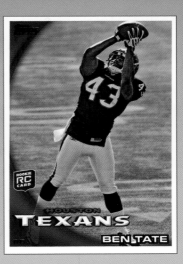

2007
Mario Williams sets a
team record with 14 sacks.

2009
The Texans have their
first winning season.

2011
The Texans reach the
playoffs for the first time.

2008
Andre Johnson leads the
NFL with 115 catches.

2010
Vonta Leach makes the Pro Bowl.

Andre
Johnson

Fun Facts

FANTASTIC FILL-IN

After the 2009 season, Matt Schaub was asked to replace injured Tom Brady in the Pro Bowl. Schaub threw two touchdown passes

in the first five minutes and was named **Most Valuable Player (MVP)** of the game.

PERFECT PICK

In 2008, the Texans selected Steve Slaton with the 89th pick in the draft. The 5′ 9″ running back was the 10th player taken at his position. That season he led all NFL rookie runners with 1,282 yards.

WELCOME HOME

When Gary Kubiak was hired to coach the Texans in 2006, it was a great homecoming. Kubiak had been a great athlete in baseball, football, basketball, and track for St. Pius X High School in Houston in the 1970s.

ABOVE: Steve Slaton
RIGHT: This trading card shows Andre Johnson wearing his old uniform.

RICE IS NICE

Andre Johnson was given number 15 when he joined the Texans in 2003. Johnson later asked for number 80. It was a tribute to his hero, superstar Jerry Rice.

TEEN SENSATION

In 2007, Amobi Okoye became the youngest player ever taken in the first round of the NFL draft. He graduated from college when he was 19 and played his first game for Houston at age 20.

WINNING UGLY

In a 2006 game against the Oakland Raiders, the Texans had a tough day throwing the ball. They actually had negative passing yardage but still won. Houston gained 129 yards running the ball, and the defense forced five **turnovers**.

NAME THAT TEAM

The Texans picked their name from a group of five possibilities. The other four were Apollos, Bobcats, Wildcats, and Stallions. More than 65,000 fans voted online to help choose the name.

"I'm just always out there trying to keep the guys pumped up, keep them in tune with what's going on."

▶ **DeMeco Ryans,** *on what it means to be a leader*

"I'm totally committed to producing a winning team, and I'm going to do everything within my power to see that we do that."

▶ **Bob McNair,** *on his championship plan for the Texans*

"I understand that it's rare in this league to go undrafted and perform at the level that I did. What people don't understand is that it didn't just happen. I worked day and night at my craft."

▶ **Arian Foster,** *on his rise to stardom*

"I've always been the more laid-back and humble guy. I don't have to be in the *limelight*."

► **Andre Johnson**, *on being a team player*

"When you throw the ball his way, something good is going to happen."

► **Dom Capers**, *on Andre Johnson*

"This is the NFL. Everybody's got good players, and everybody's capable of winning on Sunday."

► **Gary Kubiak**, *on why the Texans take every opponent seriously*

"You've got to prove your worth every week or else there will be someone nipping at your heels, ready to take your spot."

► **Matt Schaub**, *on the pressure of being a starting quarterback*

LEFT: DeMeco Ryans   **ABOVE**: Andre Johnson

Great Debates

People who root for the Texans love to compare their favorite moments, teams, and players. Some debates have been going on for years! How would you settle these classic football arguments?

DeMeco Ryans was the Texans' greatest linebacker ....

... because he was an All-Pro and played in the Pro Bowl during his six seasons in Houston. The fans called him "D-Wreck" for his hard-hitting style. Ryans was a star from the moment he joined the team. In his first game in the NFL, he made 12 tackles.

BRIAN CUSHING

Even the Texans would disagree. Brian Cushing wins hands-down ....

... because in 2011, when Houston reached the playoffs for the first time, Cushing (LEFT) was named team MVP. Before the season, Cushing actually had to change positions from outside linebacker to inside linebacker. He got used to his new job in a hurry. Cushing had 114 tackles and four sacks, forced two fumbles, and intercepted two passes. He was a Texas tornado!

Andre Johnson is the best player in team history ....

... because he was a first-class star for the Texans when they were a struggling team and a first-class star when they became a winning team. Thanks to his size, speed, jumping ability, and sure hands, Johnson was one of the NFL's few "unstoppable" receivers. He caught more than 700 passes in his first nine years with the team.

No way! Matt Schaub deserves that honor ....

... because his passing made the Texans a winning team. Schaub (RIGHT) didn't make a lot of headlines. All he did was complete passes and produce victories. When the team's running game slowed down, the Texans asked Schaub to throw more. So he went out and led the NFL in passing yards in 2009!

The great Texans teams and players have left their marks on the record books. These are the "best of the best" …

TEXANS AWARD WINNERS

WINNER	AWARD	YEAR
Domanick Williams	Offensive Rookie of the Year	2003
DeMeco Ryans	Defensive Rookie of the Year	2006
Brian Cushing	Defensive Rookie of the Year	2009
Matt Schaub	Pro Bowl MVP	2010

TEXANS ACHIEVEMENTS

ACHIEVEMENT	YEAR
AFC South Champions	2011

RIGHT: Mario Williams and DeMeco Ryans were stars for the 2011 champs.
OPPOSITE PAGE: Domanick Williams had a great rookie season for the Texans.

Pinpoints

The history of a football team is made up of many smaller stories. These stories take place all over the map—not just in the city a team calls "home." Match the pushpins on these maps to the **Team Facts**, and you will begin to see the story of the Texans unfold!

TEAM FACTS

1 Houston, Texas—*The team has played here since 2002.*
2 Southfield, Michigan—*Connor Barwin was born here.*
3 New Orleans, Louisiana—*Jacoby Jones was born here.*
4 Bessemer, Alabama—*DeMeco Ryans was born here.*
5 Miami, Florida—*Andre Johnson was born here.*
6 Richlands, North Carolina—*Mario Williams was born here.*
7 Richmond, Virginia—*Jamie Sharper was born here.*
8 Athens, Georgia—*Dunta Robinson was born here.*
9 Cambridge, Ohio—*Dom Capers was born here.*
10 Park Ridge, New Jersey—*Brian Cushing was born here.*
11 Bakersfield, California—*David Carr was born here.*
12 Anambra State, Nigeria—*Amobi Okoye was born here.*

Amobi Okoye

Glossary

Football Words
Vocabulary Words

AFC CHAMPIONSHIP GAME—The game played to determine which AFC team will go to the Super Bowl.

AFC SOUTH—A division for teams that play in the southern part of the country.

ALL-PRO—An honor given to the best players at their positions at the end of each season.

AMERICAN FOOTBALL CONFERENCE (AFC)—One of two groups of teams that make up the NFL.

CONVENTION—A very large business meeting.

DIVISION—A group of teams that play in the same part of the country.

DRAFT—The annual meeting during which teams choose from a group of the best college players.

EXPANSION CLUB—A new team that is added to a league.

FIELD GOALS—Goals from the field, kicked over the crossbar and between the goal posts. A field goal is worth three points.

FUMBLES—Balls that are dropped by the player carrying them.

HUMILIATING—Producing a feeling of shame or failure.

INTERCEPTIONS—Passes that are caught by the defensive team.

LIMELIGHT—The focus of attention.

LOGO—A symbol or design that represents a company or team.

MASCOT—An animal or person believed to bring a group good luck.

MOST VALUABLE PLAYER (MVP)—The award given each year to the league's best player; also given to the best player in the Super Bowl and Pro Bowl.

NATIONAL FOOTBALL LEAGUE (NFL)—The league that started in 1920 and is still operating today.

OVERLOOKED—Ignored or not noticed.

PHILOSOPHY—An educational field devoted to thinking and logic.

PLAYOFFS—The games played after the regular season to determine which teams play in the Super Bowl.

POSTSEASON—Another term for playoffs.

PRACTICE SQUAD——A group of players who practice during the week but do not usually play in games.

PRO BOWL—The NFL's all-star game, played after the regular season.

PROFESSIONAL—Paid to play.

REPUTATION—A belief or opinion about someone or something.

RETRACTABLE—Able to be pulled back.

RIVALRY—Extremely emotional competition.

ROOKIE—A player in his first season.

SACKS—Tackles of the quarterback behind the line of scrimmage.

SUPER BOWL—The championship of the NFL, played between the winners of the National Football Conference and AFC.

TRADITION—A belief or custom that is handed down from generation to generation.

TURNOVERS—Fumbles or interceptions that give the ball to the opposing team.

UNTESTED—Not yet proven.

OVERTIME

TEAM SPIRIT introduces a great way to stay up to date with your team! Visit our **OVERTIME** link and get connected to the latest and greatest updates. **OVERTIME** serves as a young reader's ticket to an exclusive web page—with more stories, fun facts, team records, and photos of the Texans. Content is updated during and after each season. The **OVERTIME** feature also enables readers to send comments and letters to the author! Log onto:

www.norwoodhousepress.com/library.aspx

and click on the tab: **TEAM SPIRIT** to access **OVERTIME**.

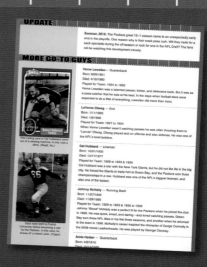

Read all the books in the series to learn more about professional sports. For a complete listing of the baseball, basketball, football, and hockey teams in the **TEAM SPIRIT** series, visit our website at:

www.norwoodhousepress.com/library.aspx

On the Road

HOUSTON TEXANS
One Reliant Park
Houston, Texas 77054
832-667-2000
www.houstontexans.com

THE PRO FOOTBALL HALL OF FAME
2121 George Halas Drive NW
Canton, Ohio 44708
330-456-8207
www.profootballhof.com

On the Bookshelf

To learn more about the sport of football, look for these books at your library or bookstore:

• Frederick, Shane. *The Best of Everything Football Book*. North Mankato, Minnesota: Capstone Press, 2011.

• Jacobs, Greg. *The Everything Kids' Football Book: The All-Time Greats, Legendary Teams, Today's Superstars—And Tips on Playing Like a Pro*. Avon, Massachusetts: Adams Media Corporation, 2010.

• Editors of *Sports Illustrated for Kids*. *1st and 10: Top 10 Lists of Everything in Football*. New York, New York: Sports Illustrated Books, 2011.

Index

PAGE NUMBERS IN **BOLD** REFER TO ILLUSTRATIONS.

About the Author

MARK STEWART has written more than 50 books on football and over 150 sports books for kids. He grew up in New York City during the 1960s rooting for the Giants and Jets, and was lucky enough to meet players from both teams. Mark comes from a family of writers. His grandfather was Sunday Editor of *The New York Times,* and his mother was Articles Editor of *Ladies' Home Journal* and *McCall's.* Mark has profiled hundreds of athletes over the past 25 years. He has also written several books about his native New York and New Jersey, his home today. Mark is a graduate of Duke University, with a degree in history. He lives and works in a home overlooking Sandy Hook, New Jersey. You can contact Mark through the Norwood House Press website.